W9-DAV-332

Journal of Modern Poetry

The 14th Edition in the Poetry Cram Series

EDITED BY CJ LAITY

ChicagoPoetry.com Press | Chicago, Illinois

ChicagoPoetry.com Press, Chicago, Illinois

ChicagoPoetry.com | PoetryCram.com | PoetryAward.org
Printed in the United States of America

Cover photo: "Sky wall" by CJ Laity

ChicagoPoetry.com has published an online poetry news source since December of 1999. It also goes by the name ChicagoPoetry.net, ChicagoPoetry.org, ChicagoPoets.net, ChicagoPoets.org, and ChicagoAnthology.com.

If you would like to learn how to get your poetry considered for a future issue of Poetry Cram, follow the guideline updates at PoetryCram.com.

TABLE OF CONTENTS

Charlotte Digregorio (pg. 88) is Midwest Regional Coordinator of the Haiku Society of America and she publishes poetry that has been translated into five languages. Her poetry is exhibited on public transit, in stores, banks, restaurants and venues where she does readings. She is also the author of four award-winning non-fiction books. She has been a professor of foreign languages and writing and holds graduate degrees from the University of Chicago.

Chris Reid (pgs. 32 and 67)) is a longtime slam poet in Chicago and has poems appearing this year in the anthologies *Rhyme and PUNishment* and *Joy Interrupted*, as well as in various print and online journals, and she is currently writing a stage play. She is a graduate of the University of Illinois.

Cordell M. Miles Jr. (pg. 98) was born in Louisville, KY, raised in Huntington Beach, CA, and currently lives in Hammond, IN.

Cynthia Pfeiffer Stell's (pg. 75) work has appeared online in T*he Melic Review, Cynic Online Magazine: Cafe Del Soul, Blue Rose Bouquet, Soul Reader* and *Poetry Victims* as well as *Poetry Cram* for which she received a Pushcart Prize nomination. She is currently working on her first book of poetry.

Deborah Nodler Rosen (pg. 73) is a widely published, award winning poet and is currently an editor of *RHINO*. She teaches poetry classes in schools under a Kids Meet Art program.

Delores Tolliver (pg. 83) is a retired City College Educator with a passion for song who has taught writing and English for 17 years. She's been published in the Journal of Ordinary Thought (Neighborhood Writing Alliance).

Dennis A. Rivera (pg. 33) is a Language Arts Teacher, an artist, a polyglot, a writer and a twenty-five-year-old student of the Catholic University of Guayaquil, Ecuador in the career of English Language for Teaching and Translation.

Diane Anjoue, (pg. 55) aka Jennifer Kress, writes poetry and short stories when she finds time amidst her busy life raising her sons with her husband of fifteen years. A sampling of her poetry has appeared in *American Open Mike, The New American Voice, The Panhandler Quarterly*, and *Sometimes We Dream*, produced to benefit St. Jude's Children's Research Hospital. While Diane isn't writing, you can find her cheering on her two baseball playing sons and her oldest son who is soon headed for the U.S. Air Force.

Diann Martin (pg. 61) is an avid reader and writer of nonfiction and poetry. She has studied at StoryStudio and at Ragdale. She lives in Wilmette with her husband and works as a nurse educator.

Don Ward (pg. 94) says he's lived most of his life "in three-piece soot: in working class New Jersey; perched atop aircraft carriers; and in corporate boardrooms among plastic-planted amazons and icy cubicles." Since retiring, he teaches Humanities electives and writing at North Carolina's Community Colleges. He holds a bachelor's degree in English and a Master of Arts in Liberal Studies from Kean University. He has published children's books, poems and non-fiction articles about technology and autism.

Donna Pecore (pg. 20) says she "is going through academic withdrawals after a 10 year odyssey culminating in a Masters from UIC" and that "she floats on the winds of chance hoping for opportunities to use her education." She says "her poetry has changed her world, saved her life, and opened her heart."

Ellen Savage's (pg. 71) poetry has been recognized by Poets & Patrons and Highland Park Poetry and has appeared in *CALYX, East on Central, Avocet*, and *The Butterfly Gardener*. Having graduated in 1976 from the University of Illinois with a nursing degree, she worked in obstetrical nursing through most of her career. After her son left for college in 2007, she began to devote serious time to writing. She is also an avid bird watcher and enjoys playing the viola and the autoharp.

Gail Goepfert (pg. 43) is a Midwest teacher, poet, and nature photographer. She has been published in a number of anthologies and journals including *Avocet, Caesura, Cram 11 and 13, Off Channel, After Hours, Florida Review*, and online at *Bolts of Silk, Prose Poetry Project, Quill and Parchment*, and *YourDailyPoem.com*. She says: "After many years in the classroom, I happily attend the school of poetry and nature."

George Korolog (pg. 93) says he "works in the left hemisphere of the world with a right hemisphere brain" and "somehow, he makes it work." His poetry has been widely published in over forty print and online journals such as *Word Riot, Naugatuck River Review, Blue Fifth Review, Poets and Artists Magazine, Red River Review, Poetry Quarterly, Riverbabble,* and *Grey Sparrow Journal*. His poem, "From tending sheep to confusion on the Amtrak 10:50" was awarded second prize in the prestigious 2011 Tom Howard/John H. Reid Poetry Contest. He was a runner up in the 2012 Contemporary American Poetry Prize for his poem, "Soul Stone" and is an active member of The Stanford Writers Studio. His first book of poetry, *Collapsing Outside of the Box*, is being published by Aldrich Press and will be released in late 2012.

Glenn Ford (pg. 76) is a poet living on the south side of Chicago.

Ismael Mohammed El-Tayuddin (pg. 74) is a Sudanese-American who teaches H.S. Mathematics and works with Special Needs and at-risk students. He enjoys writing poetry in both the English and Arabic language.

Isa Mambetsariev (pg. 64) graduated from the University of Illinois at Urbana-Champaign with a degree in English. He says: "Today I consider it to be the honeymoon stage of my love with poetry, but the love affair began when I was five years old. It all started with my grandfather who would read to me every night the works of Pablo Neruda, Alexander Pushkin, Victor Hugo, and many others. Born in a small central Asian country, Kyrgyzstan, I never saw myself ever learning English or becoming something other than a teacher at a local school. However, poetry inspired me to dream bigger and it made me realize that everyone is a poet if they can spare the time to write."

Itala Langmar (pg. 41) is an Illinois artist and has been painting and writing poetry since she was a girl in Venice, Italy. After gaining proficiency in English, she began writing poetry in English as well as Italian in the 1990s. Itala often informs her paintings with the text of her poems because choosing the right words and the perfect colors for them are mutually creative.

Jacqueline Harris (pg. 34) says she has been writing off and on throughout most of her life, toying with fiction in grade school and supernatural / horror in high school. She began writing poetry in 1999 and she says "it was in slam and performance poetry that I found my true voice." She says her poetry book *Random Acts of Verse* is the culmination of her journey through heartache, hospitalization, betrayal and ultimate triumph.

James Graham (pg. 96) has participated in poetry seminars at the Poetry Center of Chicago and he also writes fiction.

James L. Merriner (pg. 95) is a freelance writer and the author of five books about history and politics. He is the past president of the Society of Midland Authors and has taught journalism at the graduate level. He says he "has started writing poetry for the first time since he was a lovesick fool in college."

Jasminum McMullen (pg. 21) is a two time champion of Berwyn Public Library's series Poetry Idol, a mix of slam poetry and American Idol. Jas released a recording of her poetry in 2011 entitled *The Reunification of Destiny* and she is the author of the book *In My Write Mind*. She says she "writes every day and almost always on post-its."

Jennifer Dotson (pg. 54) is founder and program coordinator for HighlandParkPoetry.org.

Jenny Santellano (pg. 62) is a 45 year old mother of two working full-time as a property manager. She says: "I've loved to read and write poetry since I was a teenager but had not shared any of my poetry with others until two years ago when I joined a Writer's website. To me writing poetry is the ultimate creative outlet and helps me express the different facets of my personality."

Jim Davis (pg. 39) is a graduate of Knox College and now lives, writes, and paints in Chicago, where he edits the *North Chicago Review*. His work has appeared in *Seneca Review, Blue Mesa Review, Poetry Quarterly, Whitefish Review, The Café Review*, and *Contemporary American Voices*. He has been the winner of the Line Zero Poetry Contest and Eye on Life Poetry Prize. He can be found at JimDavisPoetry.com

JoAnne Blackwelder (pg. 49) has published poems in *The Lyric, Poet's Review, The East Hampton Newsletter, Printing News,* and the anthology *Love Notes* (Vagabondage Press). She was a runner up in *The Formalist* (aka, *Measure*) sonnet contest of 1995. She is currently organist and choir director at the First Presbyterian Church in Ocean City, NJ.

Justin Peterson says (pg. 77) "I moved to Chicago from the Pacific NW a little over a year ago. I write everyday, but am far away from being a writer. I hate doing it mostly constantly. And when I do, the webs of my fingers feel split by papercuts and the jelly of my eyes resumes to make my belly growl. Perhaps then I harbor some potential."

Kathy Lundy Derengowski (pg. 29) is a California poet who was a finalist in the San Diego Book Awards Poetry Chapbook category. She was recently published in the Ekphrasis collection *Summation IV* of the Escondido Municipal Gallery. She says "when the muse is not pursuing her—she is pursuing the muse."

Laurie Blum (pg. 56) says she "is always looking to expand her career palette." Laurie has been writing poetry and prose for several years and finds inspiration from the beauty of nature and the human condition. She says she "loves to try new activities such as sky-diving, yoga and surfing."

Linda Leedy Schneider (pg. 42) is a poetry and writing mentor and psychotherapist in private practice. She has been a faculty member at Aquinas College and Kendall College of Art and Design. Linda received the Grand Prize from 2012 Contemporary American Poetry Prize sponsored by Chicago Poetry, a Readers' Choice Award from The Pedestal Magazine, and was honored by the Dyer-Ives Poetry Competition. Her work has been published in hundreds of literary magazines including *The Pedestal Magazine, Rattle,* and *The Sow's Ear*. She has written six collections of poetry and has edited two collections written by poets whom she has mentored. Linda's latest reading was at The Saturn Poetry Series, NYC.

Lois Barr (pgs. 22 and 36) teaches language, literature, civilization and creative writing in Spanish at Lake Forest College. Her poems and stories have appeared or will appear in *Flashquake, Poetica, Phat'itude, East on Central, The DuPage Review, Mochila, Love After 70, Bedtime Stories for Everyone, The New Vilna Review* and the University of Iowa's *Daily Palette*.

Louise Mathewson (pg. 31) is an author and award winning poet who loves to write about sacred moments in the ordinary experiences of daily life. Her work has appeared in the U.S. and abroad in numerous publications, including the anthologies *Poetry Matters, Mentor's Bouquet* and the bestselling series *Cup of Comfort*. Her new book of poetry is *A Life Interrupted: Living with Brain Injury* (Pearlsong Press). Louise holds a Masters in Pastoral Studies from Loyola University, Chicago. She can be found at LouiseMathewson.com

Former college President **Dr. Lynn Veach Sadler** (pg. 30) has eight chapbooks and four full-length poetry collections and over 100 short stories published, including one in Del Sol Press's *Best of 2004: The Robert Olen Butler Prize Anthology*. She is the recipient of the Abroad Writers Competition/Fellowship (France). She has published a novella and a short story collection, has several novels forthcoming, and has written 40 plays. Now a fulltime writer and editor, she wrote all the way as she traveled with her husband around the world five times.

Marcia J. Pradzinski (pgs. 17 and 90) is a retired ELS teacher who has been published in Rhino, After Hours, Avocet, Poetry Cram and in the anthologies A Light Breakfast and Cradle Songs. She has won awards in the Jo-Anne Hirshfield contest sponsored by Evanston Public Library and in Highland Park's Poetry Challenge.

Mariah Phillips (pg. 91) says "poetry has been the main outlet for my wild pessimism this summer, and [Poetry Cram] has provided a great purpose to continue writing and functioning." Mariah also says: "Other than Harry Potter, I am fascinated by nature, by creativity, by love, and by language. I enjoy cooking and crafting, especially knitting. I knit because Hagrid, Hermione and Mrs. Weasley knit."

Marian Kaplun Shapiro (pgs. 18 and 50) is the author of a professional book, *Second Childhood* (Norton, 1988), a poetry book, *Players In The Dream, Dreamers In The Play* (Plain View Press, 2007) and two chapbooks: *Your Third Wish* (Finishing Line, 2007) and *The End Of The World Announced On Wednesday* (Pudding House, 2007). She says: "As a Quaker and a psychologist" her poetry "often embeds the topics of peace and violence by addressing one within the context of the other." A resident of Lexington, she was named Senior Poet Laureate of Massachusetts in 2006, 2008, 2010 and 2011.

Mary Chapman (pg. 46) is a wife and a mother of three grown children. She says: "My interest in writing started at the age of eighteen. However I truly developed my own style of writing years later. I started with simple poetry and have graduated to different forms including my favorites: haiku and acrostic poetry." She has had six haiku published in the online magazine *Tiny Word.*

Marianne Schaefer (M. G. Schaefer/Holoroyd) (pg. 59) says as she "grew she knew that becoming a medical professional and forensic medical specialist would not be enough for her"—even the publication of short erotica could not satisfy her need to become the erotic poet for Beast Woman Cabaret. She also created a workshop to teach the art of creative "Decadence" writing, which has been presented at the WisCon Writer's Convention, and she recently had a one-woman show at The Erotic Heritage Museum of Las Vegas, Nevada. She is currently working on a book of poetry called "Crotch Tingle" and she says she "treats patients when time allows."

Marissa Brawn (pg. 53) graduated from Loyola University in 2009 with a degree in Sociology, Anthropology, and Women's Studies. Currently, she is a Program Director at a non-profit organization in Chicago.

Mary Jo Balistreri (pg. 44) says she has met many Chicago poets through The Clearing in Wisconsin. She says: "I was originally a professional classical pianist and harpsichordist, but when my youngest grandson died, the music was not helpful in transcending grief or in giving witness to his life. I began writing poetry and have never stopped." She has been published in *Passager, Crab Creek Review, Windhover,* and *Verse Wisconsin* and she is the author of the book *Joy In The Morning* (Bellowing Ark Press) as well as the upcoming book *Gathering the Harvest.* She can be found at MaryJoBalistreriPoet.com

Mary Langer Thompson (pg. 35) is the Senior Poet Laureate for California. Her poetry appears in various journals and anthologies such as *Quill and Parchment, J Journal,* and *Off the Coast.* She is a contributor to *Women and Poetry: Tips on Writing, Teaching and Publishing by Successful Women Poets* (McFarland) and is a proud member of the California Writer's Club, High Desert Branch.

Mayi D. Ojisua (pg. 97) is a poet, painter and poetic flutist, and a graduate of Columbia College, Chicago who has had writing published in various journals and magazines. He says: "It was and still is my dream to compete with myself; to see, feel and translate my understanding of life."

Michael Schwartz (pg. 72) is 25 and lives in Aurora, IL. He says: "I started writing when I was about 14 and haven't stopped since. It's my true passion. You could say my style is unconventional. It doesn't follow any guidelines really. I just love being able to capture certain sounds or feelings."

Nancy J. Heggem (pg. 23) is a retired mathematician and a Trustee of the Palatine Public Library District. Her work has been published in the *Daily Herald, Poetry Cram, Horticulture Garden Verse,* William Rainey College *Point of View* and nine Outrider Press / TallGrass Writers Guild Anthologies. She received third prize for Automotive Poetry from the Towe Auto Museum, Sacramento, CA.

Neal Whitman (pgs. 47 and 98) says he "long ago left Chicago and headed West." He now lives with his wife, Elaine, and loves to combine his haiku with his wife's photographs, creating a combination known as haiga, and he also collaborates with his wife's Native American and Silver Classical flute.

Norman Nanstiel (pg. 48) says: "Throughout my life (starting at the age of 14) I have been writing poetry. The process of writing poetry has always helped me see deeper into the things happening around me and view life with a philosophical, and ultimately, spiritual sense that I always felt a need to share with others. The unexpected turn of a phrase or the use of a word that brings a deeper meaning with it has always given me a thrill that brings a child-like wonder to my life. I have tried to express these feelings and the lessons that life has taught me through my poetry and hope that others may be sparked into wonder through something I have written."

Pamela Larson's (pg. 78) poetry has been published in two anthologies with the Schaumburg Scribes as well as in the *Daily Herald*. She has won various awards from Highland Park Poetry for which she coordinated a 32 poet Exquisite Corpse in April 2012. Her poem Cyber Sonnet was chosen by two different artists as inspiration and was displayed with their artwork at the First Bank of Highland Park and the Lemont IL Art Center. She says she "enjoys tradition, such as trying to tackle the challenge of shortening her thoughts into haiku, but also new avenues for poetry through mixed media."

Peter Rodenby (pg. 45) is a retired engineer and a full time grandfather. He lives in an old cottage by a river with his wife and enjoys travelling, walking, dreaming and writing. His favorites are Hemingway. Nabokov, Solzhenitsyn, Quasimodo , F S Fitzgerald, D H Lawrence and the Beach Boys.

Rebecca Mullen (pg. 79) says: "I am a teacher, reading specialist, writer, and language thespian. I've been writing poems for as long as I can remember – the rhythms are in my thoughts and blood. My family wrote poems and songs for every holiday, birthday, wedding, and birth. In my free time, I live for live music. I'm an amateur photographer and a lover of this world."

Renae Ogle (pg. 63) studied poetry at the University of Tennessee and then went on to study social work. She says that "feeding my poetry helped me in helping others." She has an M.A. in English and an MSW in social work both accomplished after she turned 40. She says "I now live in Yuma, Arizona and work with veterans in readjusting to civilian life. I try to stay connected to my art (I also make turquoise jewelry) because it is very therapeutic to the therapist."

Simon Phillips (pg. 68) is an anti-war poet who has been published at RedFez.net and reviews music at WhisperinAndHollerin.com.

Renée Szostek (pg. 92) says: "I was a precocious reader, and could read when I was only four years old." She has studied at Michigan State University, Northwestern University, the University of Chicago, the University of Michigan and Yale, where she received her second master's degree. As a scientist, she has published articles in *Biochimica et Biophysica Acta, Biochemical and Biophysical Research Communications,* and *the Journal of Wound Care.* Her poetry has been published in *dotdotdash, Resist Psychic Death, Diverticulum, Cicatriz,* and previous volumes of *Poetry Cram.* She also plays a variety of musical instruments, including the piano, clarinet, flute, classical guitar, harpsichord, recorder, and carillon.

Sheila A. Donovan (pg. 57) has had her poetry published in journals, anthologies, chapbooks, newspapers and magazines and her art and poems have been exhibited at Woman Made Gallery in Chicago. She has done readings at schools, coffee houses, galleries, libraries, the Printers Ball, and the Bucktown Arts Fest and she is the originator of the annual Children's Day event for the Beach Poetry reading series. Sheila was a semi-finalist for the 2009 Gwendolyn Brooks Open Mic Award and was awarded an Honorable Mention for the 2012 Contemporary American Poetry Prize. She says: "Writing is a passion that will not permit me to lay my pen down."

Stella Vinitchi Radulescu, (pg. 89) Ph.D. in French Language & Literature, is the author of several collections of poetry published in the United States, Romania and France, including *Insomnia in Flowers* (2008), *All Seeds & Blues* (2011), and *I Was Afraid of Vowels* (bilingual, Luke Hankins translator, 2011). Her work has appears in *Laurel Review, Asheville Poetry Review, Seneca Review, Pleiades, Rhino, Louisville Review, and Spoon River Poetry Review,* and in a variety of literary magazines in France, Belgium, Luxembourg, Québec and Romania.

Terrance Raymond Carlton (pg. 70) says his "writings strive to bring unity to a segregated population through cheeky wordplay, serious social commentary, artistic line blurring, and gripping poetic promise." He currently works as the Arts & Entertainment Editor at *Gozamos*, a spotlight on Chicago community and culture. You can find him at TerryCarlton.com.

Veronica Văleanu (pg. 58) teaches English at the M. Eminescu National College in Buzău, Romania. She is a member of the editorial board of english.agonia.net, an interactive poetry website. She says: "I think my identity in writing is about being a survivivore. A poem is nothing but a frequency of the consciousness, shifting from radiating to gravitational patterns, along with the feedback of the spaces that get imprinted with this energy."

1. the scent of chicken

Congratulations go out to . . .

Best Modern Poem

"The Scent of Chicken" by Marcia Pradzinski.

2013 Pushcart Prize Nominees

Marian Kaplun Shapiro for her poem "Finding You".

Beatriz Badikian-Gartler for her poem "Packing for the future".

Donna Pecore for her poem "Transitory Mash-Up".

Jasminum McMullen for her poem "The Abandoned House".

Lois Barr for her poem "Biopoesis".

Nancy J. Heggem for her poem "Snapshot"

MARCIA J. PRADZINSKI
SKOKIE, IL

The Scent of Chicken

I watch my father bone perch at the dinner table.
　　He edges a table knife between the flesh and spine,

　lifts the body away from the skeleton
　　and pulls up the frail ladder of bones that gave

shape and structure to the fish.
　　A ladder of years separates me from my parents

but they stream back to me in the scent of alewives
　　on the lake shore sands

where my father holds my hand
　　on long Sunday afternoon strolls,

or in the heady fragrance of duck blood soup simmering
　　crusty bread baking, waiting

for a slathering of butter spread by my mother's knife
　　and a chat at the kitchen table.

Even in childbirth, my belly splayed open
　　to deliver my son,

the ghost of a memory arises –
　　I imagine the scent of chicken

but am told, *No, no cafeteria near here* by the nurse
　　as he continues to stitch and clean me.

Only weeks later when I visit a live poultry shop
　　where I went with my mother does the smell hit me,

　and I know my mother was there
　　at the birth of her grandson with her Polish blood soup.

MARIAN KAPLUN SHAPIRO
LEXINGTON, MA

Finding You

I can't find you anywhere tonight
where are you   hidden in the bone of me
hidden in the blood of me   between
my toes   in the skin that flakes off
in January   stuck in the earwax
that collects itself into dams of deafness
under salves for my splintering nails
wrecked by dry air   winter   age,
in the wrinkles (forehead, neck), freckles/
sunspots/ellipses footnotes
ibids and *e.g.*'s, *et al.'s*, rests
and repeat signs   in the dewey decimal
system of my memories which fall out
of first-apartment bookcases which didn't
come with adjustable shelves so taller
volumes have to lie sidewise, make-
shift bookends to the upright spines
more than I can count, always more, give
some away and others show up shiny
with their brandnewness.   Where are you?

                        the problem is
you are everywhere and every day you
won't sit still and I can't set
you down and I can't draw your portrait
in front of me   you keep shape-shifting
into speckles on the kitchen wall
and on my skin and into water-marks on
my stationery and into the jingling of
the Good Humor truck, all those words,
poems, songs, anything that unsays
not here

Packing for the future:
(after Lorna Crozier)

Take a pair of socks. Thick, blue or brown,
wherever you go, you'll have to walk. A velvet
pouch to hold the words, the seeds. White
underwear. Pounds and pounds of laughter
wrapped tightly in a rice paper sack. A few
golden coins, a water bottle. Just stuff
one bundle and put a stick through it, carry it
on your shoulder. Leave town walking
backwards to wave goodbye to the trees
and the neighbors. Packing for the future
requires discipline: know what you'll need
and take what you won't. Take a pair of socks,
thick and brown, leave the rest behind. Paper?
Pencils? Who needs them! Speak your stories
to anyone who'll listen. Ask them
for a chicken leg in return, a slice of raisin bread.

DONNA PECORE
CHICAGO, IL

Transitory Mash-Up

"The world is not imperfect or slowly evolving along
a path to perfection. No it is perfect at every moment,
every sin already carries grace in it." Herman Hesse

feet move to no known rules as I search for sin to play in
falling pitter patter rain an ambient soundtrack of cosmic music
bouncing riffs tickle my soul dances to "the light fandango"
castanets keep time and feet move knowing no rules

whoot whoot! she is electric vibes running hot
hotter than a summer days concrete steel reflections reign
hotter than cool jazz blowing warm vermillion boiling blues
running running running summer night sweet sweat drips
 hours past time fueled by passion's heat forced to walk on burning
asphalt cauterizes the heart one ten in the shade ten four me
ten for you to keep the beat stay in time and share
cool beans as love sprouts dust bunnies tremble
as lightning strikes thunder growls watermelon grins win

timely cooperation bringing broken parts together
where sun's heat cracked clay field to be restored
by a rainstorm's mud puddle transformation
street side splash and dash as moonlight slashes dark
 dreams suspended animation of graphic panels viewed
one at a time where a leaf floats hope on the black surface
I'm just a Zephyr of combustion filled memories
wind drifting choices to use your parachute a silk cloud

that spreads sunshine disperses dark rain clouds that rush to read
the last page accelerates the indescribable excitable
trees shake limbs as leaves rattle whisper secrets
that are not really secrets finally time to remove all doubt
find the sin is in the not the not the not
so watch the grass grow and bud's bloom, and then
clean out your closet

JASMINUM MCMULLEN
OAK PARK, IL

The Abandoned House

The windows are broken with tears that moistens the ground dirty
reflecting bits of shiny glass, web like in appearance
The thread the widow spins unraveling the love I no longer give
surrounding my feet that ache from walking with a broken heart that
sits on a sill of regret leaving gelatinous stains of unforgiving that
dries and cracks like chapped lips burning
in the place that stores fire
poked with iron, the crackling sound of my love consumed to ash
I needed the warmth so I burn all I have to make
warm again what was left frozen in open freezer doors long after
the fridge has gone out
Bulbs of light blink hesitantly dangling from a cord of hope I
pull on and off till the cord snaps in my hands the
sounds of over from your lips stick to my footsteps like stray
toilet paper, stairs I ascend to reach the door of the bedroom
off its hinges when pushed open and the sound it creaks raises
the hair on my arm as I lay on dusty covers that
smells of our love, faint but there
As I weep tears of deepest sorrow praying that God hears
Better off flies in through the shuttered window with a clipped wing
its wing tip suspended upon a shard of glass taunted by the
slight wind, threatening to fall into the depth of my swollen eye
sockets, I call out your name in the hall that echoes nothing
I am voiceless as the structure shifts quickening my descent down hollowed
stairs, My hands caked with dust from the banister that falls as
soon as it is cleaned like the love between us, diminished
I grab the knob and turn making it out as the door
slams shut latching on to its lock and I standby witnessing with
reluctance to leave the collapse of
the abandoned house

Biopoesis

It wasn't a big bang
but a series of soft
pops like champagne
bubbles bursting open
or the sizzle of
water on a fiery hot
skillet cells splitting
regenerating and
splitting again
gurgling of bubbles
buoyant bubbles
born on waves
warm magnetic
repetitive rhythmic
a sweet soporific
lullaby of creation
turned to waves
crashing on rocks
soon enough.

Banging didn't start
'til the age of stone
then God woke up
and paid attention.

NANCY J. HEGGEM
PALATINE, IL

Snapshot

I caught you there
crystalline drop
on the tip of a leaf
just after sun rise
as earth warms and
night fog creeps away.

You had traveled
across the Gulf
from the mouth
of the Mississippi,
that bore you
through twenty locks
from the green fields
of Iowa and the chalky
cliffs of Illinois,
where you lingered
as white snow blown
down in great gusts
from Canada.

It amazes me to
imagine you
joining winter rain
drops on a Koi
pond in Kyoto.

Yet, for one
split second
you are mine
alone.

2. girl crush

Womanhood

There is a strand. A strand with teeth.
I swear they're long. And sharp. Scrape my finger-combs
that try to plait—For Heaven's sake
calm down!—But they won't and strands
(with teeth) flyaway and poke in my nose, my mouth corners.
My hair-teeth chomp, eat up combs and devour my brushes
growing longer, whiter, polished
and always hungry.
They chew the rubber band holders, spitting them out.
I starved them once, those hungry
hungry pale hungry teeth.
I shaved off my hair (then the teeth they crunched they cracked),
But the neck-naked, soft-as-tongue satisfaction
grew to growling the rumbles the hunger
the long bone teeth
preyed their way back through my scalp.
I have tried I have
tried:
      braids
       buns   dyes
         clips   sprays
          ties   dryers
                  creams
      tails of pigs and ponies
But even those beast-broken-and-trained
domesticated-should-have-been-docile
fell victim to that bottomless
appetite
of those pale hungry long teeth.

Silky flowing sensuous curls
be damned.

BEATRIZ BADIKIAN-GARTLER
CHICAGO, IL

This is for the woman

This is for the woman who will not read this.

This is for the woman who is trapped inside a frame.
This is for the woman who cannot escape his words,
who cannot stop hearing her earlier voices,
who wants to be free of strings and fly,
who wants to write about others.
For the woman who hunches over fields of rice.
For the woman who escapes in the middle of the night.
For the woman who must write and requires readers.
For the woman who cannot stop the flow of time.

For all the women who need a place under the stars,
a room of their own, peace and bread.
For the women who taught me to struggle
and
for the women who listened.

KATHY LUNDY DERENGOWSKI
SAN MARCOS, CA

Geisha

Japan, with the grace of the Geisha
    Bows before her ancient lords
    The earth and sea.

She has been groomed for this-
    Their fierce angers
    And ceaseless demands.

Serving at this strange ceremony
    With soundless acquiescence
    A ritual cleansing, not unforeseen.

Shaken and shattered
    She does not lose her bearing
    The habit of poise, the pattern of control.

She will survive whatever moods they can impose
    Coax them back to civil ways
    With art and song and poetry.

Out of the chaos and ruin
    She will arise
    Mysterious, exotic and beloved.

This Geisha girl
    Japan

LYNN VEACH SADLER
SANFORD, NC

To Know a Battlefield

It's way out of Sheridan
(by some standards),
close to the site of
the Battle of the Rosebud.

The food is far beyond palatable,
but it's not what takes tourists
to the Kirby Bar.
Neither is the whiskey and such.
The draw is—

THE MEN'S RESTROOM.
We were taken there
by preeminent historian Ed Bearss,
who has the heft

to allow women in to gawk at
the trough-cum-urinal,
for the Kirby Bar does not stoop to urinals.
Ice, see, is packed on,

odors outed, ousted, tamped down (?).
Ed says you can't know a battlefield
until you stand on it.
Female, I've now stood

in the male bastion of the Kirby Bar.
I have to admit,
I ate up that history—
experienced a "right" of passage!

LOUISE MATHEWSON
EDEN PRAIRIE, MN

The Power of a Smile

Thin, soft hair, teased into a style,
glasses propped on her nose,
bent shoulders,
she stoops over a blue Sears cart
that holds her cane.
She glances up.
I meet her eyes and smile.
She returns my smile
and we've crossed a bridge,
touched souls.

CHRIS REID
CHICAGO, IL

girl crush

it's not that I go that way
but then there was this babe
with legs clear down to the floor
and she turned heads on killer heels
as she clattered her way
through the airport aisle and it's

not that I'd offer to share a cab
with her because I was heading
to the Loop as well and just
maybe to buy her a drink
as a friendly gesture
to an out-of-towner and it's

not that I would wonder
about finding a private place to
get to know her better to
flick away her bra to
peel away a scrap of lace to
let loose her snug heat

DENNIS A. RIVERA
GUAYAQUIL, ECUADOR

ERIC LOWER

Ere I met you, I thought I could love no longer
Rectifying that flawed idea I find myself now
Impossible as it sounds, I killed my scaremonger
Content as no one else can be, I take a vow
Hereby do I promise to devote my life to you
Oath to which I'll faithfully and willingly hew
For you've made me feel like no one has before
Holding my hand you've eradicated all my sore
In return, forevermore I'll give you my love
Nothing will stop me, even if push comes to shove
Eric Lower, I want you to be happy daily, monthly and yearly
No matter what befalls I'll always love you dearly

JACQUELINE HARRIS
NORTH CHICAGO, IL

Thank God for Who I am Not

You know I like being who I am.
Today anyway.
And I thank God for who I am not.

I am not a lemming:
a small rodent,
easily lead by her friends,
and her libido.
I can think for myself.
I can just as easily walk
away from the cliff
as run to it.
Besides, I am afraid of falling.

I am not a dog:
Though I do wish I had a tail
so that others could see how I felt
without me having to tell them,
I would just as soon not
sniff the posterior of others
as a formal greeting.
I would be a lonely dog.

I am not Queen of a bee colony.
I do not want to spend
my whole day in one room
getting humped by random drones
and laying thousands of nameless bastard eggs.
With wings, I would like to think
I would have better things to do.
Like flying.

So what am I?
I am a fully autonomous writer
of the female persuasion
with no husband,
and no kids,
Thank you, God!

But, I really wish I had that tail.

MARY LANGER THOMPSON
APPLE VALLEY, CA

Contemplating My Cast

Because I could not stop
for a broken foot,
he kindly bound me up—
Oscar, the cast tech.

I'm glad I got a pedicure
as he holds me steady
and wraps and wraps.
Now I'm partially mummified.

I castigate myself. Why me?
I drink green tea,
take my pills like Sally Field.
And couldn't you, Oscar,
make mine pink?

Too late.
He gives me crutches,
yet warns not to use them
until I'm home,
lest I return to his floor
with another part to be wound,
like the woman this morning.

How quickly an ankle turns,
or you meet someone
and can't walk away.
When Oscar cuts it off
I'll present it to him as a gift,
a graffitied paper nautilus
freed from my itching-to-go appendage.

LOIS BARR
RIVERWOODS, IL

We all shrink.

Pulled by gravity we sag, bend, twist.
Our defenses: gruff voices, cunning (some call wisdom),
flatulence, coarse whiskers, tough, sharp toenails.

Bigger, bolder people push us aside;
Smaller, meeker ones don't see us at all.
They trip.

Like a wine pump sucking oxygen out of a half-consumed bottle,
life desiccates our skin, our eyes, our lips.

Once grand matriarchs, we are the play toys of grandchildren:
their tiny fingers pinch flaccid folds falling from our arms.

Baroque sonnets fast forward the wizening of brows, the curve of spines,
condemning us to be nothing but earth, smoke, dust, and shadow.

Angry, we demand a second opinion
when the doctor informs us of a two inch loss in height.

Remembering the long strides of our youth, we forget we're smaller,
if only in our dreams at night.

Alas, even the tallest, once exclamation points, become commas
in the run-on sentence of life.

3. among the timbers

On Method

It begins with birds above a maple tree.

Stance: sincere expression of distaste
regarding improper use of language
concealed in commanded hypothetical

sketching its already exaggerated
orifice of the human body
as it relates to the human condition

paralleled in familiar image
turned on its head, shaken
by a drop of blood: a fury.

Reflect upon the odds
and the nature of disorder, worry
and rant about savages, who

have carved their way into history.
Scrubbed, lathered, and rinsed.
Who has not behaved improperly

when manipulating another's tongue?
Who is not a product of fusion, alive
in the smoke ring halos of the undivided?

Then again, the birds.

Nebraska Refrain

In her black dress
my daughter faces sky –

my son plants his feet
in prairie bluestem.

Echoing their childhood duets,
they keen an old country

hymn to the pinging windbeat
of a flapping awning – cover

over the vanilla-colored
casket where their grandmother

will begin her return
to the land she helped plant

and harvest, where sky
will watch over her

as she steps across
the angle of horizon.

The last notes hang
in the sun-stunned air –

my granddaughter reaches
for my daughter, touches

her tears – says,
Sing it again.

ITALA LANGMAR
KENILWORTH, IL

To a Kind Stranger

There is a big wound in the ground
In front of my house, where the old
Majestic elm stood proud,
A friend and a protector.
Last week, suddenly he was ill.
I saw his branches twist in pain while
The leaves were falling precipitously.
Brown and wrinkled, sad, moribund.
Men, professional experts, appeared
And demolished its limbs and
The glorious trunk.
Total pulverization.

A stranger stopped and spoke with
Understated sorrow about the tree
Now gone. I said to him:
It is a heavy misfortune
And a somber warning:
To have been and be no more.
I choose solitude now
But please remember
To come to my funeral.

LINDA LEEDY SCHNEIDER
GRAND RAPIDS, MI

Oak Leaves

A friend is dying

1.

I am Alyssum, the last flower alive in this planter.
It's November for God's sake, and here I am small
pure like baby's breath or bridal lace.
I bloom among the blighted.

Geranium's flare of fuchsia
is now black and curled into itself
like an infant pulls in his legs
to remember the sea.
Daisy's only eye is closed.
She holds her seeds close.

> This is Michigan- ripped by glaciers
> and soothed by the subsequent sea.
> Great Lakes wash over wounds, mastodon bones,
> Petosky stones. Sleeping Bear Dune keeps watch,
> but Lake Michigan steals sand
> with each wave and sends back snow
> to kill November flowers.

White on white, I will succumb.
November, the trees empty except for the oak
that hangs on to its dead,
carries them- brown, broken, afraid to let go.

11

My left eye hurts, waters, clouds this page.
I have sliced onions to make stock.
Soup- what else can I do when words wither,
and she hangs on brittle, crumpled,
as afraid as the Oak leaves?

(Previously published in *Pedestal Magazine, The Ambassador Poetry Project* and
in *Some Days: Poetry of a Psychotherapist* [Plain View Press 2011])

Among the Timbers

Just when I thought it was safe,
        burrs of memory nestle into once-healed flesh,
                needle tender spaces.

The slightest affronts
        mushroom into menacing territory.
                Spores thought-buried sprout.

Fogged in, the trail of wisdom
        stretches ahead unseen.
                Disquiet amplifies breath.

I stumble through the understory
        vexed by splinters lodged in flesh,
                Qualms rise, seek an opening in the canopy.

I wait for light's advent, relenting,
        listen for the fallen fruit of the hickory,
                chant the psalm of earth.

Sunset Over the Mill Pond

On the dock, a woman watches feathers of snow geese
stream across a fire-darkening sky,
red torch of sun about to burn out.
A few last flames halo treetops along the shore
and the pond becomes
a prism of muted yellows,
oranges, alizarin crimson. Swallowing silence,
a woman's breath
slows like the banked embers along the horizon.

Night blinds her until everything is sound.
A whippoorwill's repetitive call,
carp slapping against pond's edge,
a loon's cry for his mate that echoes across the water,
all tangled within the brushed voices
of memory, tucked beneath the wash of time...
She thinks of them,

her grandsons, their lives and deaths. Fireflies fall
from the trees, light up and go out, light up and go
out.
So short these signals of love.

PETER RODENBY
ST. JOHNS CHAPEL, DURHAM, UK

Yesterday I think I saw the last butterfly of summer

Yesterday I think I saw the last butterfly of summer
Exposing her wings on a late blossoming flower.
Autumn just a chilly breathe away
Winter an extended harsh memory.

Unexpected beauty of the red admiral
Resting in the warmth of October sun
Restored my faith
 Made me believe.

I can endure approaching winter
I will survive against the snow
The icy death and the numbness of despair.
Yesterday I saw a butterfly of summer

MARY CHAPMAN
ORLANDO, FL

Crescent Moon

The beauty of the crescent moon,
Waltzes in the clouds.
Whispers, descend from the mountains
Thrown against the trees are
Echoes in the night, calling for you
in the sweetness of the night air.
Of all of the things
What matters is
The way your reflection,
shimmers in the water.
I reach to touch you are not there,
only the darkness of the night.

The night has taken you away.
Keeping you from reaching out
and let me guide you back from what you have endured.
Tragically the heart could live go longer
ending its struggle to survive.
All that I remembered is,
how you looked in the light of
the crescent moon that night.

NEAL WHITMAN
PACIFIC GROVE, CA

An Idyllic Time Warp, or …

from December through April
travelers pack charter buses
overnight runs from Ohio to Florida
stiff black hats gingerly stowed in overhead bins
the bus winds its way
through hilly farm country
making pickups in small towns
we were headed to Pinecraft

white bungalows
honeybell orange trees
giant oak trees and Spanish moss
evenings almost always culminate in music
a giant cast iron-pot of elk stew
simmered on an open fire
while barefoot lead singer of the Chuck Wagon Gang
harmonized with this wife:

> *Beyond the sunset*
> *Over the sunset in that better home*
> *Angels are waiting to carry me home*

An idyllic time warp, or …
as reported in Sunday Travel,
The New York Times, April 15, 2012:
"Where Amish Snowbirds Find a Nest."

NORMAN NANSTIEL
DES PLAINES, IL

Impressions of a Still, Still Night

Not even dust is falling
Colours are asleep
No cricket, no bird, no wind is calling

The street lamp light
cast its shadows long ago
then just left them there
abandoned in their cold blank stare.

Incessantly, the tick-tick-tick
of the clock keeps haunting
each moment like the last;
even time is waiting.

Leaves on the trees
as stiff as the bough.
Motionless... just there;
Held captive by the chilled night air.

Where is the necessity of the day?
Have all our needs just passed away?
Where is want – where is greed?
The still night leaves us... just to be.

JOANNE BLACKWELDER
OCEAN CITY, NJ

Evening*

Why do we bother with the rest of the day,
the oscitancy of the morning,
the hangover aching into afternoon,

then sunset with its blast of devilish blood-orange,
its ambush of blinding swords?

This is the best—
turning on the first table lamp,
caressing the crystal decanter
and pouring that first Dewars--

maybe a hot shower and a silk caftan,
a blood pressure pill—
but mostly sipping that first golden Dewars,

dictionary and thesaurus spread by the computer,
the page of white light awaiting fingers on keys,
the TV, radio, CD player, ipod, all silent,

in the windows a darkness
empty of moon and stars
out there,
heavy clouds hurling down the flue
a snarl of wind and flinging at the house
the midnight storm.

*In answer to Billy Collins' "Morning," which appeared
first in *Poetry*, then *in Picnic, Lightning*.

MARIAN KAPLUN SHAPIRO
LEXINGTON, MA

Spring Sunlight

Green leaves growing
Photograph fading

Hair greying
Forsythia yellowing

Turtles mating
Candlestick tarnishing

Sparrow waking
me. You sleeping.

4. your half of the bed

MARISSA BRAWN
CHICAGO, IL

Your Half of the Bed

If you stay too long
your face will change.
That side has sunken
the coil, the twill, the skin cells.
You will age quickly
out of spite and tire,
jowled flesh
will make for a long expression.
Greens will become greys
with excessive wear
telling tales
of lovers passed
in the night,
I'll clutch the edge,
and when you go
my face will change.

Secret

Let me eat your secret.
Unwrap it slowly and
press it to my lips.
The taste is somewhat salty
or is it sour that I sense?
The scent is sweetened
by memory and softened
by telling. I roll the secret
in my mouth with my tongue,
clicking it against my teeth,
testing the surface for jagged edges.
I swallow the hard lozenge
of your truth and it dissolves
leaving only a bitter
breath that weighs
heavier from the burden.

DIANE ANJOUE
WOOD DALE, IL

Albatross

When the tolling of the bell
can no longer be heard
beyond the echoes in the cavern
of your empty chest cavity;
when the promise of 'until then'
stretches like a forgotten black
sand dune, littered with broken
reef litter and deadened
shore detritus;

the wingspan of the albatross
does not encompass the weight
of the grey'd sky bleak
as he picks away- searching
for crushed memories to tuck into
his hideaway- forgotten, in
his wayward nesting, the last sliver
of your dignity; stolen like a
crust of bread:

a starving writer's
last words are torn away
and forgotten.

Where Love Should Be

deep, deep,
deep beneath

{ her face}

beauty dwells
not skin deep
but to the core

{her heart}

tears fall
in
solitude
as love eludes

{her spirit}

just beyond reach
the wind stirs
a grassy whisper

{her soul}

silky soft
he murmurs her name

SHEILA A. DONOVAN
CHICAGO, IL

I WISH I WAS A PENCIL

I wish I was a pencil.
You'd hold me tightly.
When not being held by you,
I'd sit in your pocket,
embracing your heartbeat.

I wish I was a pipe.
You'd grasp me with your lips,
light me up, nice and warm.
I'd feel your breath
flowing all around me.

I wish I was your shoes.
I'd go wherever you do,
feel your toes wiggling restlessly,
caress your feet,
keep them warm.

I wish I was your pillow.
I used to be, you know.
You could rest your sleepy head.
 I would not breathe
if it disturbed you.

I wish I was your black leather couch
with rosewood arms,
or one of your oversized
paintings which dominate your walls.
You'd take pride in me, instead of destroying me.

VERONICA VDLEANU
BUZAU, ROMANIA

memory and battery

There is a sudden spark in the peel between my fingers
and I know it's about time you did something right.
The steering wheel is leading your hands into a contained heaving:
the collected reshuffle of forces
into the no-taker passing. And there's speed to
patronize the road; let it fuel us,
what remained of our passional buffer zone. Speech bubbles.
The car minimizes our voices, the musical blips
unlike the huge house where
the tones felt like untotalled. It's just a frame, don't look
and don't look sharp: sometimes
our life is where it isn't
that's where
we'll consume everything.

MARIANNE SCHAEFER
CHICAGO, IL

SOUTH OF THE BORDER

I STAYED
In a loveless marriage
In an abusive family
With a troubled teen
Holding the hands of friends fraught with fear
Because of it.

I WALKED ON EGGSHELLS
Concurrently loved and hated
In their world of black and white
Where only I saw the shades of grey
Where they begged and pleaded each day
Don't leave me

I SURVIVED
The rages and lies
The disorder and disrepair
In my personal world where
Everything was neat as a pin
Cleaned outside and in
Wielding my compulsivity like a sword

BORDERLINE PERSONALITY DISORDER
Has its own aroma of despair
Its affected travel in packs
Tearing the emotional flesh of the innocent
Leaving them open to the next attack
Vulnerable from caring and loving
Able to deny the elephant in the room or the monkey on their back

I DON'T LIVE IN THEIR ZOO ANYMORE
I PREFER TO LIVE SOUTH OF THE BORDER

BRENDAN THOMAS
YORKVILLE, IL

Tawny Thin

I held the young body—
The clean, beach-bound,
Tight-jeaned,
New-to-cocaine body.
Through unbuttoning,
I released the sandy body of now,
Smooth and fragranced.
Then, with open apertures,
Using methods of model spending,
I freed the body—
Tousled and satisfied.

DIANN MARTIN
WILMETTE, IL

Waiting for your driver's license to be mailed back

Since you can't be designated to do the driving (designated driver)

maybe you can be the designated darling and go around smiling and laughing and making up bad pickup lines in front of all of the young women who are in anticipation of every word that comes out of your mouth and then text you afterwards to see what might be in it for them or…

maybe you can be the designated douche bag and piss off everyone and try to find a way to stick it to them even when they least expect it or maybe laugh your ass off at their antics in real time or maybe you would like to be the designated dreamer -

Who sighs a lot and wonders what the world holds in its big bag 'o tricks next and likes to be lazy and sit back and think about it

Or you may be lucky enough to be the designated dear one who holds people and their hearts in the palm of your hand like egg shells and keeps them from breaking into a gazillion tiny pieces with quiet wisdom and peace

Or maybe, just maybe- you can learn the subtle, sneaky and unknowable reason that you are a human being and not a softshellcrab.

JENNY SANTELLANO. GLENVIEW, IL

Lassoed

Soaked in solecism
Cast out and chewed off
Fancied, forlorn, forgotten
Pushed out of bounds without penalty

Imprisoned in a world of wanting,
carelessly he makes his move;
malevolent, morose, manipulator

Cognitive and cunning she
thwarts his arrows...
Six bullets to the back and head

Presumptuous was he, to assume
there was no fee

RENAE OGLE
YUMA, AZ

Vomit

He thinks its okay that he comes here,
that he drops hints that he's not
   gonna stay with her.

it makes me feel sick that
there could be thoughts
being entertained from

any direction that i could
ever even consider any kind
of entanglement with

my ex-husband.

I think I threw up
a litte bit
in my mouth.

ISA MAMBETSARIEV
CHICAGO, IL

Love in a letter

There are no syllables to love,
No little wordings to amaze.
Love simply is a coward's lust,
It lives in simplest of ways.
And all too soon it waves and wanes,
A symbol of our dying youth.
It stands and snickers while we lie,
In bed, alone, too cowardly to praise
The beauty that true love is
True to pain.

5. the street writes a poem

CHRIS REID
CHICAGO, IL

Visitation on the South Side

With valuables stowed in the car
I shuffle through the metal detector
and sit with the 5:30 group
before being herded downstairs
to where the prisoners stage

I assess my nephew
after twenty-seven months in jail
his eyes look pretty clear
but there's new damage to a front tooth
or maybe I didn't notice it before

He talks fairly loud
to drown out the goddaming around us
He thanks me for the history book
and coming to court for status call
He says he had a dream of me

I do not tell him he was in my dream too
We lean in
our hands instinctively in opposition
on the smudged Plexiglas
I tell him I miss him and turn to leave

I want to keep my dream to myself
he and I walking late through the city streets
At Hyde Park I stop to point
to the place the O'Neills once lived
but add there was never any music there

CATHLEEN SCHANDELMEIER
AND SIMON PHILLIPS
CHICAGO, IL / LONDON, ENGLAND

SUBWAY VACATION
A collaboration for Chicago Calling.

Beautiful view
back of the train
Penthouse Suite on the CTA
Conductor announces
GET AWAY FROM THE DOORS
the train is packed
I don't even notice
from my glass bubble
in the back
I am in relaxed spacial heaven
-with a view!-
my first-time experience
with the upper crust
who need not dirty their hands
to clean
or want for space, food, money
Have never stood packed on a train
like fish food
No comprende
Those who struggle daily
just to stay alive

suddenly full of guilt
self-loathing
for my moment of relaxation
I have a vice gripped
around my chest of
anger and injustice
about to jump out of my skin!
I wonder at the calm indifference of the
Blonde
well-heeled
woman
beside me reading her e-book.

Wonder what she's reading
I can't ask, just imagine
something set in the loop
Killer being chased
Down a Iron fire escape

Jumping to the sidewalk
Gunshots fired as he races away
Running up Damen
Flat Iron in the distance
Crashing into artists carrying canvas
Reverie broken
By the El stop chime
got to get to work song
abrupt end to my
Subway vacation.

TERRANCE RAYMOND CARLTON
OAK PARK, IL

"N.E.R.D."

I forget more than I produce, but here's the truth:
The persistence of memory is hemorrhaging,
and everything we know and love
must come to an end or subsequently suspend.
Counteractively, no one ever really dies.
That's N.E.R.D. for those of us who don't mind.
Unwind and find
a particular binding agent that's authoritative and undermined.
Get us where we need to go once and for all.
Some of us will rise while the rest of us will fall…
…And justice for all!

ELLEN SAVAGE
HIGHLAND PARK, IL

Going To the Poetry Reading

The train station's door spits
me out where clots of people
congeal in the failing light.

Wheelchair-bound and legless,
a man grins as my head swivels
to gauge construction-clogged traffic.

To escape the concrete's fever, I flag
the nearest taxi pointing toward the library,
climb into the blast of its merciful chill.

As I pull the door shut, an unintelligible language
spews from the radio. *State and Congress,* I say.
The driver affirms with "Fertile Crescent" accent.

The cab feels like a protective membrane
as it surges forward, a corpuscle crammed
into a vast circulatory system.

My pulse pounds as the cabbie alternately stomps
the gas then brakes, zigzagging,
squeezing by an eyelash. I suck air

through clenched teeth; he finds the bus lane
and floors it; at the intersection we burst free
like an embolus zeroing in on the brain,

a pedestrian races for her life,
my mouth goes talcum-dry,
hands in rigor mortis on the seat edge.

Pulling to the curb outside the library, I consider
dialing the cops, but instead tip well,
grateful to be a survivor.

MICHAEL SCHWARTZ
SUGAR GROVE, IL

ABSTRACT ASTERISKS

These accolades seamlessly activate an arbitrator
to facilitate a wager on a dull debate.
Cemented in dense subjects at the expense
of an entrenched public's amendments of a frivolous penance.
As renegades went away to generate a mistaken
invasion to agitate the restraints that regulate.
That extends to degrees of tenths which dispenses
infamous legends with defenses against unnatural elements.
Along with abnormal instigators waving notifications
against the weighted strangulations by a vacant administration.
Whether concessions through a severance or recessions
with consequences, Congress' collections remain relentless.
Trying to infuse a motivation to medicate an accumulation of outrage
or speculate over failures as they lacerate and coagulate.
Finding remnants of pensions that commences insurrections
as a remembrance of increments in possessions.
Fierce concentration as dissuasion dissipates and persuades
to replace fabrications with faithful postulations.
Final connections to the mechanisms that implements the suppression
to the dependence that dissents the decrepit directives of false premonitions.

DEBORAH NODLER ROSEN
GLENCOE, IL

THE STREET WRITES A POEM

The street is sincere, dark and straight,
pays no attention to the buildings staring at it.
The street lies flat, does not return
the glares of the glass windows.

Street lights shine down. Cars hulk
one behind another. The street holds up
the green car, the red car, the silver
which all look the same from underneath.

The street ignores the wall on its east side
as patiently as it ignores the buildings to its west.
The wall has attitude. The wall has art – screaming
mouths, bulging eyes, red streak of lips,
but the street does not have time to consider art.
It must lie flat ceaselessly day and night.

The wall can demean the street, its dull blackness,
but despite its screaming mouth and bulging eyes
red lips and dreams of fame, it depends on the street,
cannot risk the street's withdrawal as it plots
year after year to assert its independence.

The 1st Ruku of Hajj

(The first bow of the Muslim Pilgrimage)

Shoulder to shoulder, Humbled before that same Power

Fearful of that same Hour

We realized that our lives,

had been united by that same Dawah

Facing the light, beautifully we stood, swaying slightly in winds like flowers planted

Souls listening to sacred words chanted

hearts appreciative of favors taken for granted

Cheeks wetted................. as the chests of men panted

sins regretted................... errors recanted

Silence falls.....................then...bodies submit to what was commanded

Millions strong.........before Allah.............. with our backs slanted

CYNTHIA PFEIFFER STELL
OAK LAWN, IL

broke:
a found poem: from overheard conversations,tv,radio

tonight's story will focus on
it's the car again
unexpected expenses
or the dryer
the hell with vampires, i'm afraid of
if you need a bankruptcy lawyer
any reason why your payment was late
school loans
even with the deductible
it's not the worst that could happen
recently laid off
stimulus package
i got your stimulus package right here
i don't wanna ask dad you ask dad
gave themselves bonuses
we need that money for
man, can't even afford generic generics
family-owned businesses going under
unpaid furloughs
selling their
houses or walking away
abandoning pets
tax cuts for the
oil spill, invasion and another invasion
billion trillion gazillion
no time and a half no overtime
it has come to our attention
so if we get the car fixed
this bill this bill this bill and this bill
brother can you spare a
brother can you spare a
and tomorrow we take a look at
it's the car again
unexpected expenses

GLENN FORD
CHICAGO, IL

THE ILL ONE

like dogs they wonna keep me muzzled
   cuz many of my pieces are missin' from the puzzle
somehow my elevator didn't rise to the top
   nuts and bolts rusted in my biological clock
somewhere down the line it just stop tickin'
   I was goin' coo-coo as this piece was bein' written
birds chirpin' i hear voices
   and I smell terpen tine as i inhale
c uz my mind is off the wall
   i'm on the brink of insanity a fall
and now shrinks got me on respodall
   an anti-psychotic
cuz lyrically i'm hypnotic
   in a trance a daze
and there's no snappin' out of it
   turn page after page cuz I love it
I'm mentally ill on this microphone
   I'm mentally ill and all alone
somewhere out in sing-sing
   you have to be there to understand
what i mean

JUSTIN PETERSON
CHICAGO, IL

Streetlamps Matter

Watching the kettle as windshields melt away
Some guy's socks get thicker in the a.m.
Boots stay tied all day on the site
Feet smelling worse when the days end
Getting ready to see her again
Somehow it still stays fresh
Sidewalks feel better every year
On them they chase breath
The whiskey they drink swims better in winter
Thought he was done with Winston's
But in the chill
They always be tasting better
Streetlamps never more watchful
Blown copper glow lights their movie in that scene
Where you first took his cigarette out his lip
Your eyes settled like eruption ash
Blowing smoke over his left shoulder side
Dragged it again and he really didn't mind
He kept thinking how he wished you had no coat
So I could feel like a man and give you mine
You may have talked of wonder
But it's the silence he'll keep inside
That's what it is to be ageless
Knowing there is no other night
Like the one cloaking you
The shield against
Time's war across worlds
Keeping us two out of sight

Red

they called her
even though the dye
faded years ago

She made no promises
but her timing
was as dependable as Monday

She kept a secret like Vegas
gossip killed by clinking ice cubes
and the word Cheers

Drinks were bought on her tab
destroying pocket evidence
grabbed for by snoopy spouses

As the Cinderella hour struck
she shook her keys into order
left like a Pastor at the end of service

stepped into never ending night
A lottery chanced statistic
death shouldn't play with guns

Tears rolled behind strobes
painful flashes of departure
sorrow spread onto the street

Wilted flowers lay where she did—
cigarette butts and time
covering the fade of red

REBECCA MULLEN
EVANSTON, IL

guild and gun

Already picturing what this poem may become
City noises…a guild and gun.
Of love and life
   coming undone
Anonymity taking flight
storming passionately
through this life
no more country views
except on my drive home
winding crossroads
lead me where I roam.
Putting on my cape and crown
and the day-to-day paraphernalia
that I've found.
Cleaning the spider webs
collected from year to year.
Should have seen it more
clear-ly
or remembered it a bit
more vivid-ly
through my arched doorways
and creaky floors.
I am whole again
    once more.
Guess I better lose another piece
    and explore.

ADAM BENAVIDES
COLUMBUS, WI

Ode to Midnight in Milan

There is a feeling in Milan
That's hard to forget.
Storied and beautiful buildings under shimmering lights
Are seen every night as you venture
Through the narrow streets on your way home.
Whether it be by train, tram or trolley,
The city speaks to you.
Vibrant conversations full of laughter, drink and music
Escort your thoughts as you walk over glistening cobblestones
Laying as the floor of a Piazza built hundreds of years before.
The sound of a roaring Vespa engine in the distance
Bounces off ancient brick
As you catch the eye of a beautiful woman dressed in black.
She is an eerie angel, perfectly dawning precious peacoat.
Milan is like your friend.
And all you must do is listen.
As I approach the bridge in the horizon,
I walk over the reflecting canals,
Surrounded by the cacophony of a satisfying Saturday night.
Leaning over the ledge and looking out,
I exhale a drag of a hand-rolled cigarette,
And begin to smile

CAMILLE ROSE CASTILLO
WEST HAVEN, UT

Beyond The Looking Glass

Though I clearly see
Paralleling traits
Corresponding facets
Astonishingly quaint

This complex, albeit moving
Prominent connection
Holds a minute blemish
Worthy of reflection

Contrast, yes there's one
A distinction can be drawn
For you're rarely right
While I'm never wrong!

Allow me, if you will
Just one final venture
Aside the playful banter
This afterthought, don't censure

 Of different roles, diverse tasks
On dispersed, divided paths
Thoughts are firmly fused
Beneath our layered masks

Yes, beyond the looking glass
Lies mystic, certain likeness
Disengaged, detached
Yet baring sharp resemblance

A vision all-consuming
So strikingly familiar
Is seemingly my own
Essence fiercely mirrored

CASEY DERENGOWSKI
SAN MARCOS, CA

The Class Reunion

Forty years have elapsed since college graduation
Twenty-six members had set a date to return
Some had earned recognition as professional successes
While two gained notoriety as convicted felons
Some had died of most natural causes
One had died by his very own hand
Despite plastic surgery, age had exacted a price
No one recognized Ted, the athlete, for his chubby cheeks and paunch
Marlene, the model, was disguised by her many wrinkles
Olga, a ballet aspirant, now pirouettes her obesity
Macho Man Mason, now thin as a rail, depends on oxygen
Wanda wears a wig, Travis sports a toupee
Dennis has a problem with his loose fitting dentures
Harriet's hearing aid whistled throughout the meal
Grayson looks most professorial with his full, grey beard
Benedict is as bald as a tonsured monk
Valerie, class valedictorian, suffers the lingering result of a TIA
Cynthia, a former wallflower, is now Cyndi the charmer
Scotus, the scholar, was brimming with irrelevant information
Clifford's cane got caught between two chairs
I also was there, but no one took note
Some had been blessed with the passing of years
While others had reasons to shed many tears.

DELORES TOLLIVER
CHICAGO, IL

"Cause My Daddy's Gone"

Did you know my daddy, Ray, if you didn't it's a dog gone shame.
He could sing like a humming bird, moved his feet as he drummed the beat.
Daddy's gone, gone, he's been gone so long.

Oh he had such a zeal for life, loved the ladies 'especially late at night.
Didn't mean any harm at all, just loved to charm them with his flirty songs.
Now he's gone, no more mellow sweet love poems.

I remember the tunes he'd pluck, that my brother often sang! Dad could
make such pretty music, could create a picture while I sat on his knee.
When I think now he's dead and gone, leaves a pain deep inside of me.
My daddy's gone, gone, he's been gone so long.

When I think of my dad's love, and the way he would laugh with me.
When I feel like I want to cry and the sadness grips hold of me. I just sing
this song, 'cause my daddy's gone, he been gone so long.

6. nest of days

ANNE WESLEY
LUBBOCK, TX

Meditation

True story: last night I dreamed I haunted
an oceanside house filled with sand drifts and
whisperings of hushed regrets.
The walls were weepy driftwood
bowed and warped and splintering
my fingertips as I groped my way through
unfurnished and salt-streaked rooms
colonized by dear-johns I'd slighted
and old lovers I had carelessly stung,
come to collect on my conscience's debt.
I tried to undress my long skirted sorrow,
as if contrition were garments to shed
or redress could be sewn up by apology only.
Then the house
sighed on its hinges,
flung wide a window,
shuddered and groaned
a tone poem born
of the vast nearby Sea
frothed and nudging tenderly
to summon fresh its first memory
with a whoosh: to forgive
to let go, to be friendly and soft
hearted, warm; to let peace murmur in
with the tide, to remit
the damages done
and pardon us all.
Then the wind dwindled to low humming lilt,
familiar and brisk and filling my palms with a palpable heat.
I unghosted the halls, unlatching doors, and quietly crooning
these words of absolution for the loafers and pokes
who were dawdling. They could stay at their will
or go when they would: I told them this treaty will hold,
and it did. Yes, even on waking.

Drifting

At the greasy spoon,
flames rise from the grill.
I relish my promotion.

I look out into twilight.
Across the highway,
fog settles over steel tracks
in frozen ground.

I should have left by rail
decades ago, rather than drift
in rain, leaving no footprints.

Living on flat land,
I dream of dazzling ocean,
strewn with rocks and lighthouses,
guarded by emerald peaks.

In my corner, the waitress
interrupts my musings.
She serves joe, tepid and watery,
in a bottomless cup, as the smell
of corn dogs wafts from another table.

Sky darkens,
moonless, starless.
I hear the grinding
on the tracks.

STELLA VINITCHI RADULESCU
CHICAGO, IL

War Face

I saw it smiling I saw it blue
and crying

who lost a leg an arm should praise the sun—
louder the voice

smaller a life

the cock keeps crowing the day keeps coming:

it's called nostalgia the old obsession
with colors and sounds

while living—the fabric shrinks   not
to compare to other things like plastic birds

& plastic stars   the TV on   I shiver:
so much to die so many times

a war at home
another coming and all the tears all the excitement

I wish
to be in the middle

I wish to be at large
I wish to be buried with my boots on:

a holy scene with puppets and guns
no more dreams

nobody sleeps

MARCIA J. PRADZINSKI
SKOKIE, IL

nest of days

a pigtailed girl skips backwards
her mother yells you'll split your head open
water paints shadows on a concrete shore
a father's bent fedora flips off in the wind
raucous laughter drifts into the nausea of a cigar
a sister tugs locks into stay-still submission
an infant suckles

those images lie dormant
and when they stir
beak-starved and ravenous
with twigs tangled
they braid new tales –
a mother skipping backwards
a pigtailed girl muttering open your mind
lake water breaking open the concrete shore
to swallow the fedora worn by the infant
who chews on a cigar and locks
the door to the past

MARIAH PHILLIPS
MONEE, IL

A lonely, jobless, hopeless college graduate's ode to her blanket

Oh, fuzzy microfleece,
Your light warmth makes me miss
My absent friends: their faces,
Their clothes, and most of all, embraces—
Proof that they were real
And that Former-Me, at least, could feel.

I know that you don't have emotions,
But since you're here, you can mop the oceans
Standing in my eyes.
I can hardly verbalize
What it means,
O Thou-of-Well-Sewn-Seams,
That you are here for me when there's no sun or moon.
You're kind of dirty though. I should wash you soon.

Positive Thinking

If a man were born

    Without hearing

       Without sight

          Without smell

            Without taste

              Without touch,

He would be a delicate human, to be sure—

But who could ever break his heart

RENÉE SZOSTEK
SCOTTS, MI

Dreaming

At night,
things were never what they were during the day.
I wandered among the trees, in the moonlight,
feeling their bark.
So rough and scaly sometimes,
that I could have almost torn off a piece
and kept it.
Other times, smooth and satiny and soft
yet tight, like my face after I had washed it in the morning.
The trees cast enormous shadows,
larger than any real tree, even a sequoia.
I wandered among the shadows with my thoughts.
They were curious bats,
flying in and out of the shadows.
It was so quiet
I could hear the scraping sound
of a crumpled, fallen leaf
as the wind blew it along the sidewalk.
In the summer, I could hear
the rustling of leaves
as they slid against one another
in the breeze before a storm.
In the winter
it was even quieter.
I had only the crunch of
my feet in the snow
to accompany my thoughts.
I was in the space between sleeping and waking
like the space between thinking and writing,
where everything seemed unreal,
and yet everything was possible.

GEORGE KOROLOG
WOODSIDE, CA

Imagining Heaven
(For Christine Hall)

Honest to God, it used to be
        that there
    was such a thing as empty space.
        Empty
as in vacant of thought, of mind, of ideas,
        hearts without hope,
        sightless in a seeing
    world. Not anymore. Were you listening?
Have you heard? Nothing is now
        teeming with implausible amounts of
        something. I'm not talking about debris, or
        about tiny left over bits of dust
here, perhaps a random molecule or
        two caught with nowhere to go, left hanging
        in space like forgotten toys in the attic
        after we have moved to a fine new house.
I'm thinking Ray Bradbury, Asimov,
        Captain Kirk beseeching Spock to turn in
        his chair, facing the computer and asking
        it to chime in about reality.
Working. Now, it seems, our old empty space
        is full of particles popping in and
        out of being, sparklers, coming from
        nowhere, dangling around for a micro
millisecond, going somewhere, which is
        back to nowhere, like new popcorn without
        kernels, bursting from the empty flat of
        the pan and then disappearing halfway
up the pot. Who would have envisioned that?
            I bet you couldn't have predicted this
            any better than Faust expected that he
            could fly from Berlin to Singapore in ten
hours. Now, I'm imagining matter being
        created by thought. Here's a blue apple
        with antlers. If our imagination is infinite,
        then whatever we can imagine is a thing
already there, waiting. It does make me
        wonder. If we can imagine heaven, then
        it must already be here.
        Working.

DON WARD
RALEIGH, NC

The Getaway

The best place to hide from a distaff world is Mars
where the atmosphere is mostly carbon dioxide.
Obviously the inhabitants are automobile-friendly.
Revving engines and the periodic whine of power tools
render conversations delightfully inaudible.
Temperatures on that planet range from a balmy eighty degrees at noon
to a bracing one hundred below at midnight.
That's great for night skiing.
The Red Planet is coated thick with dust.
And since there are many active volcanoes,
occasional manly verbal outbursts go unnoticed.
Venusians don't know "Klaatu barada nikto" means: "ESPN available here."

JAMES L. MERRINER
EVANSTON, IL

Postcards from Hell

1.
You are not known here—
I have asked all I meet—
So it is safe for you to come.
Bring only gold coins
And small-caliber weapons.

2.
Mama died and left us a bundle
So we are seeing the world.
Do you mind if we crash with you
On Friday? We'll bring
The ukelele—and bonbons!

3.
Thought you would want to know
The rumor is going 'round here
That you have forgotten
Your humble origins.

4.
After the apocalypse we must
Return to the forest and live
On roots and berries and the flesh
Of small mammals. I for one
Look to you for leadership
In this matter.

JAMES GRAHAM
WILMETTE, IL

Edge

You need to somehow
Find the strength
To make your muscles
Move just a little

You need to somehow
Find the will
To face the terror
Of the day to day

You will your nerves
Forcing electric current
Through the resistance
To trigger some action

You blink your eyes
Listen to the hum
Of the universe
Calling out

You feel a cool wind raise you
To your knees
Tectonic plates shift
Buildings crumble

Rivers run backwards
As you stand up
Straight
And tall

MAYI D. OJISUA
CHICAGO, IL

Senses

Deaf music played
by blind children,
brings pleasure to those who cannot see,
the mask of human emotions.

Echoes of drums,
for the deaf can dance,
to whom the deaf can't ask,
to tell the story of their feelings,
rising like waves in the ocean.

Blank passages illuminating
the corridor of reasoning,
we passionately move up and on.

The sun comes up
and shines between the rooms.
The sun sets behind the moon.
The blind, have only the picture of one night.

CORDELL M MILES JR.
HAMMOND, IN

My Means:

I may not always do right
And at times I may search out wrong
But beneath it all
Beneath the beast
The beauty calls
So if the end justifies the means
Then my means
Will end me where I belong

NEAL WHITMAN
PACIFIC GROVE, CA

Truth Be Told

are is
you are is less
where you are is less a
knowing where you are is less a science
perhaps knowing where you are is less a science than
an act of faith

ChicagoPoetry.com Press

Made in the USA
Charleston, SC
04 October 2012